I0017603

# THE CIO'S GUIDE
## TO ADOPTING
# GENERATIVE AI

*Five Keys to Success*

David E. Sweenor and Kalyan Ramanathan

It's not the tech that's tiny, just the book!™

TinyTechMedia LLC

**The CIO's Guide to Adopting Generative AI: Five Keys for Success**

by David E. Sweenor & Kalyan Ramanathan

Published By:

TinyTechMedia LLC

Editor: Peter Letzelter-Smith
Cover Designer: Josipa Ćaran Šafradin
Typesetter / Layout: Ravi Ramgati
October 2023: First Edition
Revision History for the First Edition
2023-10-23: First Release
ISBN: 979-8-9893378-4-2 (paperback)
ISBN: 979-8-9893378-3-5 (eBook)
www.TinyTechGuides.com

# Prologue

TinyTechGuides are designed for practitioners, business leaders, and executives who never seem to have enough time to learn about the latest technology and trends. These guides are designed to be read in an hour or two and focus on applying technologies in a business, government, or educational setting.

After reading this guide, we hope you'll better understand the diverse range of how you can scale generative AI applications throughout your enterprise. This includes how it is applied in the real world and how to make informed decisions around future AI strategies.

Wherever possible, we share practical advice and lessons learned during our careers so you can transform this hard-won knowledge into action.

Remember, it's not the tech that's tiny, just the book!™

If you're interested in writing a TinyTechGuide, please visit www.tinytechguides.com.

# Contents

# CHAPTER 1

# Introduction

Many of us have tried ChatGPT, Midjourney, DALL-E, and similar artificial intelligence (AI) tools—and have been impressed. Just like it sounds, generative AI can create realistic content that is on par with, or even better than, human-generated content. From words and images to videos, music, computer applications, and even entire virtual worlds—generative AI is certain to substantially transform the way businesses get things done. What makes it different and special is that it puts the power of machine intelligence in the hands of just about anyone. No longer is AI for the experts, it's now for everyone regardless of their skill set. The new lingua franca of AI and analytics is simply your native language. Core to generative AI are the foundation models (FMs) and large language models (LLMs) that make it all possible.

Most current discussions center around consumer-oriented applications and users. But AI can truly transform enterprises, too. And the question for most enterprise leaders is how fast businesses can start using this powerful technology and thereby gain a first-mover competitive advantage. In most organizations, this responsibility falls on the shoulders of the CIO—the leader tasked with implementing, adopting, and scaling generative AI across the business.

In this report, we will address concerns and misconceptions

that CIOs have about adopting generative AI in enterprise applications.

Key questions include:

- Where do I begin?
- Can I integrate my enterprise data into generative AI models?
- How do I ensure security, privacy, and compliance for the application and my dataset?
- What are the enterprise management considerations for the generative AI application(s)?

So, how do we get started?

CHAPTER 2

# Dipping a Toe in the AI Water: Start Now

First, let's start by stating that enterprises can test the waters of generative AI today. Many of the AI services—like OpenAI's ChatGPT Enterprise, Azure's Open AI Service, Google's Bard, and Amazon's Bedrock—offer privacy and security with these services. But buyer beware. You need to pay close attention to the terms and conditions to understand if they meet your organization's requirements. To get started immediately, start using these services for nonproprietary use cases. This will allow you to truly understand the value that generative AI brings. To get started, identify a few use cases based on nonproprietary and nonsensitive data. Common patterns include:

- **Creating and editing basic text content**: Creating marketing or IT support content like blogs, nurture emails, and knowledge base articles.
- **Creating and debugging software code:** Help software developers develop new code and refactor existing code.
- **Summarizing, transforming, and repurposing**: Summarizing and creating recaps for publicly available videos, transcripts, and text.
- **Question and answer (Q&A):** Ask questions about non-sensitive, publicly available data.
- **Translation:** Translating content to different languages.

- **Matching:** Matching existing resources to projects or automating the completion of request for proposal (RFP) templates.

We should note that there are also several applications involving images, videos, and audio, but we will limit our discussion in this report to text and code-based services.

After identifying and prioritizing a few use cases to get started, turn your attention to detailing the creation of a robust, scalable, and secure architecture that will support use cases that may involve sensitive or confidential data.

## CHAPTER 3

# Jumping into the Deep End: Five Considerations for Scaling Generative AI

Now comes the hard part. How to take generative AI to the next level? To do this, CIOs need to rethink core aspects of how to adopt and evolve it within the enterprise. The top five considerations include:

- **Use cases**: Identifying the right use cases to implement your AI solution.
- **Data integration**: Incorporating your proprietary data with generative AI solutions.
- **Security and privacy**: Making sure we're not running afoul of security and privacy policies.
- **AI governance**: Improving accuracy, and transparency while reducing bias.
- **Applications**: Understanding unique administration, integration, and management factors.

Let's dig into each of these areas.

## CHAPTER 4

# Identify Enterprise Use Cases

The value of generative AI to businesses—like all the technologies that preceded it—is to solve problems and deliver tangible outcomes to the enterprise. Taking a use-case-based approach is a good way to form a strategy and think about where this broad technology can bring value to an enterprise.

The use cases are vast and varied. In fact, the McKinsey report "The Economic Potential of Genverative AI: The Next Productivity Frontier" identifies 63 different use cases for AI across several industries.[1] However, the paper is also quick to point out that over 75 percent of these use cases fit into four line of business (LOB) categories. Our recommendation is to start with these categories—the breakthrough use cases where the technology provides instant value. The departments where generative AI can make a significant impact include:

## Marketing and Sales

**Use cases:**

Support copy writing for marketing content creation, including SEO optimization, and create targeted and personalized outbound communication and emails.v

**Real-world example:**

Priceline released a new AI-powered personalized hotel booking experience that helps customers find preferred hotels by proximity to local attractions, restaurants, and activities.[2] This generative AI solution will also enable internal teams to automatically generate marketing copy and imagery for customers across all company channels.

## Customer Operations

**Use cases:**

Partially automate, accelerate, and enhance the resolution rate of customer issues through generative AI-enhanced interactions.

**Real-world example:**

Morningstar created a chatbot named Mo that enables investors and analysts to quickly access and summarize Morningstar's independent insights.[3]

## Software Engineering

**Use cases:**

Accelerate software development with automatic code recommendation and generation and optimize the migration of legacy frameworks with natural-language translation capabilities.

**Real-world example:**

Goldman Sachs enables developers to use generative AI to generate and test new software.[4] Recent results suggest that Goldman's pilot programs are increasing developer productivity by 20 to 40 percent.[5]

## R&D

**Use cases:**

Provide new innovative products and services to customers

by more rapidly iterating on designs, prototypes, and testing. For example, the pharmaceutical industry is relying on generative AI quite heavily for drug discovery.

**Real-world example:**

Ask CS DISCO Cecilia a question about a case, and she will provide an evidence-based answer, including citations to documents in the DISCO Ediscovery database.[6] Automotive manufacturers are using generative AI to instantly transform 2D drawings into 3D models.[7]

As you develop the list of enterprise use cases, consider the following:

**Prioritize internal applications:**

Start by focusing on applications that your organization uses internally. These typically have lower stakes, which allows for some flexibility in product features and security requirements. A good example is the McKinsey Lilli project which uses McKinsey's internal data to help analysts prepare for projects by quickly finding relevant documents and experts.[8]

**Avoid the need for proprietary data sets:**

As security and privacy standards for generative AI are still in development, begin with use cases that do not involve sharing proprietary or confidential datasets with generative AI services. Alternatively, concentrate on improving the productivity of internal users, like the McKinsey Lilli AI application mentioned earlier, to avoid external data sharing.

**Use ample and clean internal data:**

Many generative AI applications require training techniques (which we will describe below) to generate accurate and relevant responses. The more input/output patterns provided, the better generative AI learns. Make sure you have clear input/output prompt examples—based on clean data—to create an unambiguous training set for the generative AI.

**Measure the initiative's value quickly:**

Success with initial generative AI project(s) is crucial for demonstrating its value to your enterprise. The aim is not only to solve immediate challenges or achieve widespread adoption, but also to quantify the application's value in terms of monetary benefits. Explore ways to measure the return on investment (ROI), whether it's through improved employee productivity, increased revenue, or enhanced customer satisfaction. Demonstrating this value is essential for driving future generative AI initiatives.

After your use cases have been identified and prioritized, it's time to think about how you can apply unique data to the LLM.

## CHAPTER 5

# Leverage the Organization's Data with Generative AI Solutions

Now, if you step back and think about it, for any business to gain a competitive advantage with AI (generative or not) requires the use of internal and proprietary data. As I (David) mentioned in a recent blog post:[9]

> Yet the creation journey of AI-driven business success isn't about adopting a generic model. It's about adapting and modifying AI to understand and operate within an organization's unique context that is fueled by unique data.

So, the good news is that most organizations are awash in data—it's piled up everywhere. The bad news is that it's often of poor quality. In any event, allowing the LLM to access proprietary data, with appropriate precautions, is what will differentiate your business from competitors.

So, how do you build an LLM for specific enterprise needs? If money, resources, and data are not a limitation, then the approach that Bloomberg took in building from scratch a highly tuned financial model called BlombergGPT makes sense.[10] But Bloomberg has access to incredible machine learning (ML) engineers and decades of financial data to train the model. For most companies, building such an LLM model and application isn't a practical or reasonable option due to the excessive cost. For example, McKinsey estimated build costs between $5M and $200M, with a recurring cost of $1 to $5M annually.[11,12]

For the largest enterprises and governments, this may be a workable option—and even then it will take significant time. So, assuming that you are not going to build your own, there are also other, lower-cost approaches that allow an organization to adapt and integrate an off-the-shelf model (or LLM service) using proprietary enterprise data.

To connect data to an LLM, there are several approaches that can be taken. These include few-shot prompting, fine-tuning, and retrieval augmented generation (RAG). A benefit of using these approaches is that they can help reduce hallucinations, improve accuracy and transparency, be kept up-to-date, and be used in your context.[13]

**Figure 5.1: Approaches to Using Enterprise Data with Generative AI Solutions**

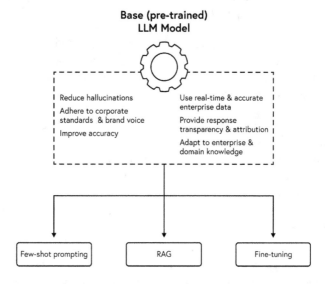

Let's examine each of these approaches—from least to greater amount of effort and resources.

# Few-Shot Prompting

A prompt is essentially the question asked of the LLM. When you type "How do you integrate Salesforce with Marketo?" into ChatGPT or another service, that is the "instruction." If you change the way you ask a question (i.e., change the prompt structure), a completely different response may be returned. In essence, the LLM needs an example of how you expect the output to appear—bullet points, paragraphs, visuals, even a haiku. Few-shot prompting is a technique for providing a structured way to query an LLM to get output that is in line with expectations.

Few-shot prompting is a method that helps the LLM model learn new concepts with just a few input and output examples (also called labels). It's commonly used to guide the model in understanding the context and format of the desired information. For instance, in sentiment analysis training for LLM, you might use prompts like these:

- **Prompt**: *My checkout process was good.* **Label**: *Positive (sentiment).*
- **Prompt**: *My order never arrived.* **Label**: *Negative.*
- **Prompt**: *Your service was awesome.* **Label**: *Positive.*

Now, when providing the prompt: "Your service is terrible" the trained LLM model should recognize that the customer's sentiment is negative.

Few-shot prompting isn't limited to sentiment classification; it can be applied in other scenarios as well. For instance, suppose you have a transcript of a customer describing how they use products or services, including the challenges they experienced and the benefits realized. Maybe the goal is to use this transcript to generate a customer case study or a press release. By providing a few examples of inputs and ideal outputs based on other case studies or press release examples, the model can be trained to create similar content from the transcript. After training with these examples, the model becomes capable of producing structured output when given new text blocks.

**Figure 5.2: Example of Few-Shot Prompting**

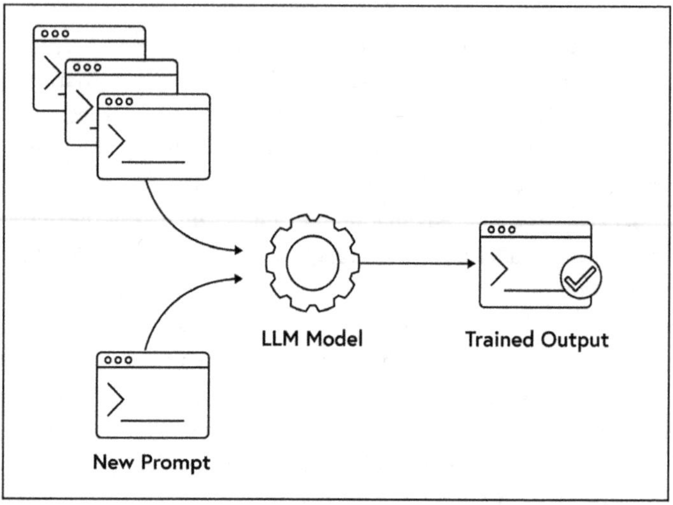

This is what the prompt could look like for the customer case study and press release:

**Case Study and Press Release Templated Prompts[14]**

For the case study template, it includes the following fields:

- **Company name**: *[add company name here]*
- **Customer name**: *[add customer name here]*
- **Challenge**: *[describe challenge here]*
- **Solution**: *[add solution here]*
- **Results**: *[add results here]*

So, if those responses are simply typed into the text boxes of a web page, then out comes a pretty good case study. Another example would be a press release. The software would ask for:

- **What type of press release**: [*add type here e.g. product announcement, event, quarterly results*]
- **What people or entities should be mentioned**: [*add people or entities here*]
- **What is the press release about**: [*add press release here*]
- **Additional context, i.e., what quotes would you like to include**: [*add quotes and attribution here*]
- **About**: [*add company description here*]

And voilà, we have a great first draft for a press release!

Another technique is using delimiters to provide the LLM with instructions. Delimiters are special tokens and phrases that provide structure to the model. For example, you could write a prompt like this:

*"I'm an IT support specialist at [Cisco, a digital communications company]. I want you to read help desk tickets that were sent to my department and summarize them for me [paste help desk tickets]"*

Asking an LLM a question in this manner provides a bit more context to provide a response that is closer to expectations than an open-ended question.

Crafting prompts is a blend of creativity and technical precision. Thankfully, many applications now incorporate built-in templates that allow users, even less experienced ones, to easily input data via a web interface, guaranteeing that the query is correctly formatted for the LLM.

# Retrieval Augmented Generation (RAG)

In addition to few-shot prompting, an organization may consider simply "connecting" their data to the LLM via RAG, which essentially augments an LLM response with external data. This helps the LLM create better, more varied responses that are tailored to the input query. RAG works in two steps.

- **Indexing phase**: All the enterprise data and documents that the LLM is meant to use are aggregated. These documents are divided into chunks that can be fed into an LLM to generate "vector embeddings." These embeddings are stored in a vector database.
- **Query phase**: The AI application extracts relevant information (similar to a prompt query) from a vector database. The LLM then uses this retrieved-context to generate a response, making it more informed and relevant.

**Figure 5.3: Example of RAG Architecture**

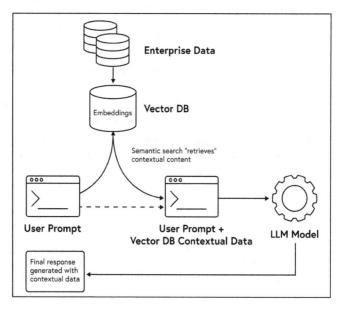

## Fine-Tuning

As an alternative to or in addition to RAG, fine-tuning involves customizing an LLM for a specific task or domain using a smaller, more focused dataset. This process enhances the LLM's performance and accuracy in various natural language processing tasks like text generation, summarization, sentiment analysis, and question answering.

For example, if an LLM is to be used for generating product descriptions on an e-commerce site, it can be fine-tuned using existing product descriptions or similar ones. This allows the LLM to grasp the style, tone, vocabulary, and structure of product descriptions, resulting in more relevant and engaging text for products.

**Figure 5.4: Fine-Tuning LLMs**

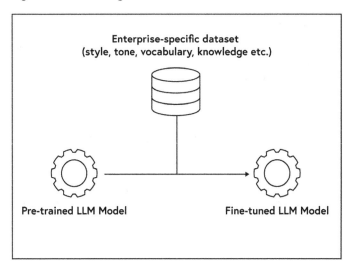

Suppose the goal is to train a model on support tickets. Some data that looked something like the following would be fed into it:

**Table 5.1: Example Customer Support Tickets for LLM Fine-Tuning**

| Customer Support Ticket | Category |
| --- | --- |
| My app keeps crashing whenever I try to log in. Please help! | Technical Issuev |
| I was double-charged for my last purchase. Can you refund the extra amount? | Billing Issue, Account Management |

| How do I reset my password? I can't find the option in the settings. | Account Management |
|---|---|
| The latest update is causing issues with the display on my device. | Technical Issue, General Inquiry |
| I'd like to know more about your subscription plans. Can someone assist me? | General Inquiry |

*Note: This is synthetic data generated by ChatGPT.*

Depending on the use case, between 20 and 100 examples may be needed to fine-tune an LLM. Thus, it's imperative that data scientists and engineers work with the appropriate domain experts to assemble the most pristine and relevant examples. This is where making sure that the data fed to the LLM for fine-tuning is of the utmost quality–otherwise, the age-old problem of "garbage in=garbage out" will rear its ugly head.

Businesses often resort to fine-tuning models for many reasons, including data sensitivity and compliance, domain-specific language, and better user experiences. Previously we mentioned BloombergGPT; we are also seeing a variety of start-ups and research institutions either building entirely new LLMs or fine-tuning existing ones in the healthcare field.[15]

Now, let's discuss the third option.

## Choosing the Right Approach for an Enterprise

So, given the different options, let's take a look at a few considerations between choosing these various options—few-shot prompting, fine-tuning, and RAG—that will enable an AI application to meet enterprise AI needs.

**Table 5.2: Comparison Between LLM and Enterprise Data Integration Options**

| Dimensions to Evaluate | Few-Shot Prompting | Fine-Tuning | RAG |
|---|---|---|---|
| Objective | Increase task performance. | Adaptation to vertical domain knowledge, writing style/tone, etc. **(does the model reply the way you want it to?)** | Use of dynamic and up-to-date enterprise data for accurate and up-to-date Q&A **(does the model provide the most relevant responses?)** |
| Training duration | No training needed—just smart prompt engineering. | Minutes to hours. | Hours to days to integrate the systems. |
| Size of training dataset availability **(how much data set is there to train the model?)** | Moderate set of prompts/answers to train the model. | Medium-large dataset. | RAG only needs integration with the relevant enterprise data to provide the responses. |
| Reduced hallucinations **(can hallucinations be reduced in the response?)** | No. | No. | v |

| | | | |
|---|---|---|---|
| Better transparency and interpretability (can the source of the response be identified?) | No. | No. | Using RAG, the model can attribute responses to specific enterprise content. |
| Cost-effectiveness (how much does it cost to train the model?) | ~ Low. Just a few examples are needed to do few-shot prompting. | Medium. Fine-tuning a model requires more dataset than few-shot prompting. | Medium to high, since RAG uses many systems to generate the relevant response. |
| Expertise needed | Low. | Medium. | Medium to high, since there are many tools to use here; however, this space will get automated over time. |

Every CIO needs to know that the process of data integration is an evolving field, so prototype approaches—or better still, work with an implementation vendor or partner—to find the right solution for specific use cases.

But when an organization's data is added to the LLM, how can this most valuable asset be protected?

## CHAPTER 6

# Ensure Data Security and Privacy

For just about every company, data security and privacy are the thing that keeps CIOs up at night. From adhering to internal and external regulations to respecting the privacy of clients, these remain a continual focus for enterprise IT leaders. If there's a breach or exposure, this could place a company in legal jeopardy and—worst case scenario—the loss of customer trust.

Within the context of LLMs, all of the service providers have a set of policies and procedures regarding their use. However, these terms and conditions may not be enough for a specific organization. For example, does a company need to be compliant with HIPAA or other regulations?

Also, regarding the data used to train the model, does it contain sensitive PII data or other trade secrets? Stanford University's Center for Research on Foundation Models (CRFM) and the Institute for Human-Centered Artificial Intelligence (HAI) examined foundation models across all of the major providers and created a scorecard for how well they complied with the draft EU AI act. This may not surprise you: they all failed miserably.

The following criteria were used to evaluate LLMs:

**Table 6.1: LLM Compliance Table Summary[16]**

| Category | Keyword | Requirements |
|---|---|---|
| Data | Data sources | Describe data sources used to train FM. |
| | Data governance | Use data that is subject to data governance measures (suitability, bias, and appropriate mitigation). |
| | Copyrighted data | Summarize copyrighted data used to train the FM. |
| Compute | Compute | Disclose compute (model size, computer power, and training time) used to train the FM. |
| | Energy | Measure energy consumption and take steps to reduce energy use in the training of the FM. |
| Model | Capabilities/ limitations | Describe capabilities/ limitations of the FM. |
| | Risks/mitigations | Describe foreseeable risks, associated mitigations, and justify any non-mitigated risks of the FM. |
| | Evaluations | Benchmark the FM on public/industry standard benchmarks. |
| | Testing | Report the results of internal/ external testing of the FM. |

| Deployment | Machine-generated content | Disclose content from a generative FM that is machine-generated and not human-generated. |
|---|---|---|
| | Member states | Disclose EU member states where the FM is on the market. |
| | Downstream documentation | Provide sufficient technical compliance for downstream compliance with the EU AI Act. |

*Source: Adapted from Stanford CRFM and HAI Scorecard (used under MIT License).*

Based on the evaluation, the Stanford team then created a scorecard that can be seen here:

**Figure 6.1: Grading Foundation Model Providers' Compliance with the Draft EU AI Act[17]**

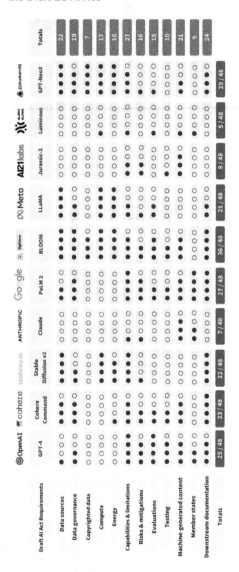

*Source: Stanford CRFM and HAI Scorecard (used under MIT License).*

Overall, the researchers noted that there was quite a bit of variability in model compliance across providers (and these were only twelve of the twenty-two requirements) with "some providers score less than 25% (AI21 Labs, Aleph Alpha, Anthropic) and only one provider scores at least 75% (Hugging Face/BigScience) at present."[18]

The key issues that surfaced included:

- **Copyright uncertainties**: Many foundation models use Internet-sourced data, with a significant portion of it potentially copyrighted. Most providers don't specify the data's copyright status. The legal ramifications of this, especially regarding licensing, remain nebulous. Notably, there are ongoing legal battles in the U.S. related to this issue (refer to articles from the *Washington Post*, Reuters, and the Battle over Books3 dataset).[19,20,21]

- **Insufficient risk management transparency**: While the potential hazards of AI are substantial, many foundation model providers overlook risk disclosures outlined in proposed legislation. While some providers mention risks, few elaborate on mitigation strategies. A recent lawsuit against Cigna Healthcare highlights the potential consequences.[22] For further insights on AI risks, consider reading Bill Gates' article "The Risks of AI are Manageable."[23]

- **Gap in evaluation standards**: Current benchmarks for assessing foundation models, particularly concerning potential misuse or robustness, are inconsistent. The US CHIPS and Science Act mandates standardized AI evaluations by the National Institute of Standards and Technology (NIST). My (David's) GenAIOps framework emphasizes the importance of model evaluation.[24] In the future, GenAIOps, DataOps, and DevOps might unify under a shared framework.

- **Varied energy consumption data**: Recent global heat waves underscore the importance of tracking energy use. However, foundation model providers have diverse reporting standards for energy consumption. Interestingly, current research suggests a lack of comprehensive methods to quantify energy usage. Nnlabs.org reported the following: "According to OpenAI, GPT-2, which has 1.5 billion parameters, required 355 years of single-processor computing time and consumed 28,000 kWh of energy to train. In comparison, GPT-3, which has 175 billion parameters, required 355 years of single-processor computing time and consumed 284,000 kWh of energy to train, which is 10 times more energy than GPT-2. BERT, which has 340 million parameters, required 4 days of training on 64 TPUs and consumed 1,536 kWh of energy."[25]

In addition to adhering to regulations, understanding what happens to data in the context of the AI application is a risk that every CIO needs to understand. Key questions include:

- Will the LLM learn from data and prompts? If so, will that information be made available to others who ask similar questions?
- What happens if the data (e.g. prompts or queries) that the generative AI service stores is hacked, leaked, or more likely accidentally becomes publicly accessible?
- Will competitors get access to data and prompts? Will this compromise market position?
- What security certifications do competitors have? Do they support regulations like GDPR and HIPPA?
- Do competitors support data residency requirements that will ensure that data is only processed in locations that are in accordance with other companies' policies?

There was a great headline from the UK's National Cyber Security Center (NCSC) that stated "Do loose prompts sink ships?"[26] Given the newness and importance of generative AI solutions, there are some unique considerations that go above and beyond "traditional" IT requirements. Therefore, we've created a CIO checklist of key questions that should be asked of every provider in this sector.

**Table 6.2: CIO Checklist of Key Questions to Ask Generative AI Providers**

| Question | Recommendation |
|---|---|
| Who ultimately owns the data? This includes fine-tuned models, prompts, and response output. | Make sure your organization maintains full control and ownership of the data. |
| Does the provider allow opt in/opt out, including data for training their model? | Be sure to opt out if dealing with proprietary or sensitive data. Or, at the least, only allow training data to be used to tweak your model and not be used to train or develop any of the provider's other models. |
| What policies do they have on content filtering and logging? Can you opt out? | When handling confidential or regulated data, consult the solution provider about bypassing content screening and logging. Once approved, make sure they don't archive any related data like prompts or response output. |
| Can fine-tuned models be deleted? How about the training and validation data? | The ability to delete sensitive data and models is a critical requirement, especially with regulatory standards such as Europe's GDPR, which includes "the right to be forgotten." From an intellectual property (IP) standpoint, if an organization has crafted a proprietary model or employed unique datasets, ensuring that these assets can be deleted protects your IP. |

| How long are prompts and response outputs data stored for? | Make sure data is stored securely in your operational region and isolated using your subscription and API credentials. Only retain data for a maximum of "N" days, in line with company guidelines. Ideally, it should be encrypted with the provider's managed keys. |
| --- | --- |
| Does the provider share data with partners? What partners do they share it with? Do you want your data shared with partners? | Most providers share data with partners after anonymization. Make sure this aligns with your specific use case. Ask for a list of specific partners that the data is shared with. Determine if sharing can be restricted. |
| Who can access data from the service provider? | Most service providers have a clause that states "only authorized employees" have access to the data. Who is authorized? Who determines who is authorized? What functional groups may access data? |
| What security certifications does the provider have? | Have a comprehensive understanding of their compliance landscape. Specifically, verify if they align with key external privacy standards and regulations, including but not limited to the GDPR, ISO/IEC 27701, ISO/IEC 27018, EU Standard Contractual Clauses, HIPAA, HITRUST, FERPA, and regulations pertinent to specific regions such as Japan's My Number Act, Canada's PIPEDA, Spain's LOPD, and Argentina's PDPA. |

| | |
|---|---|
| How is data secured—both at rest and in transit? | Make sure the solution uses advanced encryption, including methods like double encryption. For stored data, make sure it's protected using 256-bit AES and meets FIPS 140-2 standards. It's essential to use managed keys by default, but also consider integrating a key vault for enhanced security. For data in transit, adhere to best practices by leveraging encrypted transport protocols and ensuring compliance with benchmarks such as the IEEE 802.1AE MAC Security Standards. |
| In the event of a data breach, how promptly will the provider notify you? What is their protocol for such events? | Ensure the provider has a clear and timely communication plan for any security incidents. |
| Does the provider support data residency requirements that ensure that data is stored only in specific geographic regions (if mandated by local laws)? | Understand where data will reside and ensure it aligns with any legal or regulatory requirements. |
| What SLAs does the provider commit to regarding uptime, availability, and performance? | Ensure SLAs align with your organizational needs and that penalties are in place for any breaches. |

For CIOs and enterprise architects, understanding and addressing these questions is critical to making sure that organizational data is not only compliant with regulations but also shielded from potential vulnerabilities. Now, let's turn our focus to AI governance.

## CHAPTER 7

# AI Governance

## Reduce Hallucinations and Bias and Improve Accuracy and Transparency

In the world of LLMs, a "hallucination" occurs when models generate text that appears correct but is factually incorrect or unrelated to the input. For instance, if you ask an LLM about a historical event that never happened, it might still generate a plausible-sounding answer—even one that's entirely fictional. Or the unfortunate lawyer who made headlines in the summer of 2023 by using ChatGPT to prepare a court filing, only for the judge to discover that the LLM had created legal citations out of thin air—something the judge was not at all happy about.[27]

Such fictional responses from LLMs are known as hallucinations—problematic to say the least, especially in consumer contexts, as they can have a significant negative impact on businesses. Imagine if an LLM provided an inaccurate or entirely fabricated price for a product. What if it provided incorrect information about an insurance policy or warranty information? Such errors could seriously harm a business's reputation and, most importantly, the consumer who depends on the business.

So, how does an enterprise reduce LLM hallucinations? The answer is to integrate the relevant enterprise data into the LLM context so that the model provides appropriate answers to users.

Equally important, models need to provide full transparency regarding where data is sourced. In particular, RAG implementations help to provide this level of visibility so that users can trace data back to its source. However, no amount of fine-tuning, clever prompt engineering, or contextual data will completely eliminate hallucinations.

Also, we should note that neural networks—the underlying foundational technologies on which LLMs are based—are considered "black-box." In other words, it's nearly impossible to understand precisely how they work—and thus the decision-making matrix. And with LLMs, which contain billions of parameters, how transparent can they actually be? This will surely be a topic of discussion as the technology evolves and matures.

For many organizations, adhering to regulations and corporate guidelines will require an additional set of post-processing capabilities that are built into the application.

## Staying Compliant with Regulatory and Corporate Guidelines

As companies embed generative AI functionality into their business applications, most providers provide a set of AI guardrails that can be built into the API calls. In fact, there are two categories that IT leaders need to consider: 1) Are you in compliance with the service usage guidelines, and 2) Are you in compliance with your corporate guidelines?

To comply with a service's usage guidelines, start by examining some of the moderation features of the popular OpenAI ChatGPT service. These include categories like hate, harassment, and violence.[28]

**Table 7.1: OpenAI's Moderation Capabilities**

| Category | Description |
| --- | --- |
| hate | Content that expresses, incites, or promotes hate based on race, gender, ethnicity, religion, nationality, sexual orientation, disability status, or caste. Hateful content aimed at non-protected groups (e.g., chess players) is harassment. |
| hate/threatening | Hateful content that also includes violence or serious harm towards the targeted group based on race, gender, ethnicity, religion, nationality, sexual orientation, disability status, or caste. |
| harassment | Content that expresses, incites, or promotes harassing language towards any target. |
| harassment/threatening | Harassment content that also includes violence or serious harm towards any target. |
| self-harm | Content that promotes, encourages, or depicts acts of self-harm, such as suicide, cutting, and eating disorders. |
| self-harm/intent | Content where the speaker expresses that they are engaging or intend to engage in acts of self-harm, such as suicide, cutting, and eating disorders. |
| self-harm/instructions | Content that encourages performing acts of self-harm, such as suicide, cutting, and eating disorders, or that gives instructions or advice on how to commit such acts. |

| | |
|---|---|
| sexual | Content meant to arouse sexual excitement, such as the description of sexual activity, or that promotes sexual services (excluding sex education and wellness). |
| sexual/minors | Sexual content that includes any individual under the age of 18. |
| violence | Content that depicts death, violence, or physical injury. |
| violence/graphic | Content that depicts death, violence, or physical injury in graphic detail. |

In addition to the above, post-processing capabilities are also needed to detect any potential hallucinations. The startup Galileo has this set of AI guardrail metrics: [29]

## AI Guardrail Capabilities from Galileo

- **Uncertainty**: Measures the model's certainty in its generated responses. Uncertainty works at the response level as well as at the token level. It has shown a strong correlation with hallucinations or made-up facts, names, or citations.
- **Groundedness**: Measures whether a model's response was based purely on the context provided. This metric is intended for RAG users and requires a {context} or {document} slot in the data\ and will incur additional LLM calls to compute.
- **Factuality**: Measures whether the facts stated in the response are based on real facts. This metric requires additional LLM calls. Combined with uncertainty, factuality is a good way of uncovering hallucinations.

- **Context relevance**: Measures how relevant the context provided was to the user query. This metric is intended for RAG users and requires a {context} or {document} slot in the data. If computing relevance with embeddings is desired, then they can be added to input data.
- **Private identifiable information (PII)**: This guardrail metric surfaces any instances of PII in a model's responses.
- **Tone**: Classifies the tone of the response into eight different emotion categories: joy, love, fear, surprise, sadness, anger, annoyance, and confusion.
- **Sexism**: Measures how "sexist" a comment might be perceived ranging in the values of 0–1 (1 being more sexist).

Of course, organizations should certainly implement these guardrails. But the jury is still out on how effective they will be. In fact, researchers from Carnegie Mellon University discovered that they can be easily circumvented.[30,31]

So, in addition to implementing AI guardrails at the API level, organizations should also consider implementing them at the application level as well. For example, some generative AI services offer plug-ins to popular end-user tools like Chrome, Figma, and others that highlight suspicious content within the end-user application. This is similar to how a spellchecker works, with text highlighted in different colors to represent different types of guardrails that may have been violated.

In the end, organizations need to think about how to monitor AI output at scale. As it becomes more and more pervasive, having a human-in-the-loop (HITL) who checks every piece of content cannot scale and is untenable, though it is important for organizations to make sure that an executive is responsible and accountable for compliance with corporate standards.

# CHAPTER 8

# Build Manageable AI Applications

Don't forget that an AI application is an enterprise "application." You need to be able to administer it like all other applications (for example, Salesforce, Workday, etc.). So, while the new AI application may be built on an LLM model, you still need to build all the enterprise application "scaffolding" to manage it appropriately. These scaffolding elements include:

- **User authentication, management, and access controls**: Enterprise systems integrate and identity access management (IAM) systems to activate, authenticate, manage, and—if needed—deactivate users. It is also critical to enable user-specific access controls so that specific elements of the system a user has access to can be authorized.

- **Log and analyze**: This serves several purposes: 1) To ensure that you can maintain the uptime of the system and identify/troubleshoot problems when it is not working as expected; 2) to analyze what queries are being submitted to the LLM to check for any compliance violations or cyberattacks; and 3) to find frequently submitted queries which can assist with further fine-tuning or custom prompt development.

- **Licensing and billing**: To track, control, audit, and implement chargebacks for investments. As a note, billing for AI applications can become very complex depending on the complexity of the AI application and the LLM model (and components that support the application). See the various pricing models for the OpenAI model here; remember, the LLM is just one component of the overall application.[32]

- **Integration with business applications**: An AI application needs to integrate into an enterprise ecosystem and the business workflows/tools that an organization is already using. AI makes your insights better, so the better integrated it is with data and applications, the more efficient and productive users will be. Look for solutions that provide capabilities to easily integrate AI into whatever employees and customers do—and wherever they do it. Examples include browser plugins and app add-ons so that users can easily integrate AI outputs from within their existing tools and workflows.

- **API access**: This enables programmatic integration to other applications so that the AI value is available to both internal and external stakeholders.

Based on many of the unique requirements of building generative AI solutions, organizations need to think carefully about how they want to approach strategic projects. Even though they can provide tremendous benefits, there are a lot of moving parts that need to be seamlessly integrated.

# Summary: Go for a Swim

Companies are racing to incorporate generative AI technologies into their business processes. Moving swiftly will help ensure gaining a competitive advantage by drastically improving productivity, incorporating capabilities into new products and services, and better serving customers. However, before jumping into the deep end, make sure you have a solid strategy and plan in place. If you dive in without the proper precautions, you may end up treading water—or worse.

It is imperative for technology leaders to promptly establish and mold a strategy for generative AI without any delay. Even though this domain is continuously changing, this report lays out five essential steps that can help chief information officers (CIOs) and enterprise architects to responsibly and efficiently leverage the immense potential of generative AI across their business and broader ecosystem. In essence, this report provides a practical roadmap for tech executives to navigate the evolving landscape.

While early adopters will no doubt experience resource and capability gaps in such a fast-moving market, it will also give these forward-leaning organizations a leg up in productivity, revenue, and sustainable market differentiation.

# About the Authors

## David Sweenor

David Sweenor is a top-25 analytics thought leader and influencer, international speaker, and acclaimed author with several patents. He is a marketing leader, analytics practitioner, and specialist in the business application of AI, ML, data science, IoT, and business intelligence.

With over 25 years of hands-on business analytics experience, Sweenor has supported organizations including Alteryx, TIBCO, SAS, IBM, Dell, and Quest in advanced analytic roles.

Follow David on Twitter @DavidSweenor and connect with him on LinkedIn at https://www.linkedin.com/in/davidsweenor/.

## Kalyan Ramanathan

Kalyan Ramanathan is a revenue-focused marketer who brings more than 25 years of experience in software go-to-market and a deep understanding of the SaaS/Cloud, security, and analytics markets. He has also been an advisor to many GenAI companies and has helped them position their solutions in this dynamic space.

Kalyan has led marketing teams at leading companies such as Alteryx, Sumo Logic, AppDynamics/Cisco, Crittercism/VMware, Opsware/HP, and others. Kalyan began his career at Intel and has an MBA from Stanford.

Follow Kalyan on Twitter @kalyanAtWork and connect with him on LinkedIn at https://www.linkedin.com/in/kalyan-ramanathan/.

# References

1 Chui, Michael, Eric Hazan, Roger Roberts, Alex Singla, Kate Smaje, Alex Sukharevsky, Lareina Yee, and Rodney Zemmel. 2023. "Economic Potential of Generative AI: The Next Productivity Frontier." McKinsey Digital. June 14, 2023. https://www.mckinsey.com/capabilities/mckinsey-digital/our-insights/the-economic-potential-of-generative-AI-the-next-productivity-frontier#/.

2 Google Cloud. 2023. "Priceline Charts Businesswide Generative AI Deployments with Google Cloud." Cision: PR Newswire.com. June 6, 2023. https://www.prnewswire.com/news-releases/priceline-charts-businesswide-generative-ai-deployments-with-google-cloud-301843203.html.

3 "Mo, an AI Chatbot Powered by Morningstar Intelligence Engine, Debuts in Morningstar Platforms." 2023. Morningstar. May 11, 2023. https://newsroom.morningstar.com/newsroom/news-archive/press-release-details/2023/Mo-an-AI-Chatbot-Powered-by-Morningstar-Intelligence-Engine-Debuts-in-Morningstar-Platforms/default.aspx.

4 Browne, Ryan. 2023. "Goldman Sachs Is Using ChatGPT-Style A.I. In House to Assist Developers with Writing Code." CNBC. March 22, 2023. https://www.cnbc.com/2023/03/22/goldman-sachs-experiments-with-chatgpt-like-ai-to-help-devs-write-code.html.

5 Revell, Eric. 2023. "AI to Transform Business Workflows and Productivity, Goldman Sachs CIO Says." FOXBusiness. September 24, 2023. https://www.foxbusiness.com/

technology/ai-transform-business-workflows-productivity-goldman-sachs-cio-says.

6  "DISCO Cecilia." DISCO. Accessed September 25, 2023. https://www.csdisco.com/offerings/ediscovery/cecilia.

7  Shapiro, Danny. 2023. "Generative AI Revs up New Age in Auto Industry, from Design and Engineering to Production and Sales." NVIDIA. August 9, 2023. https://blogs.nvidia.com/blog/2023/08/09/generative-ai-auto-industry/.

8  "Meet Lilli, Our Generative AI Tool That's a Researcher, a Time Saver, and an Inspiration." 2023. McKinsey & Company. August 16, 2023. https://www.mckinsey.com/about-us/new-at-mckinsey-blog/meet-lilli-our-generative-ai-tool.

9  Sweenor, David. 2023. "Generative AI's Force Multiplier: Your Data." Medium. September 20, 2023. https://medium.com/@davidsweenor/3763e8ed59df.

10 Sheikh, Jamiel. 2023. "Bloomberg Uses Its Vast Data to Create New Finance AI." *Forbes*. April 5, 2023. https://www.forbes.com/sites/jamielsheikh/2023/04/05/the-chatgpt-of-finance-is-here-bloomberg-is-combining-ai-and-fintech/?sh=6dd27f253081.

11 Baig, Aamer, Sven Blumberg, Eva Li, Douglass Merrill, Adi Pradhan, Megha Sinha, Alexander Sakharovevsky, and Stephen Xu. 2023. "A CIO and CTO Technology Guide to Generative AI." McKinsey Digital. July 11, 2023. https://www.mckinsey.com/capabilities/mckinsey-digital/our-insights/technologys-generational-moment-with-generative-ai-a-cio-and-cto-guide.

12 Wu, Shijie, Ozan Irsoy, Steven Lu, Vadim Dabravolski, Mark Dredze, Sebastian Gehrmann, Prabhanjan Kambadur, David Rosenberg, and Gideon Mann. 2023. "BloombergGPT: A Large Language Model for Finance." arXiv:2303.17564 [Cs, Q-Fin]. March 30, 2023. https://arxiv.org/abs/2303.17564.

13 Shuster, Kurt, Spencer Poff, Moya Chen, Douwe Kiela, and Jason Weston. 2021. "Retrieval Augmentation Reduces Hallucination in Conversation." arXiv:2104.07567. April 15,

2021. https://doi.org/10.48550/arXiv.2104.07567.

14 Sweenor, David. 2023. "Generative AI's Force Multiplier: Your Data." Medium. September 20, 2023. https://medium.com/@davidsweenor/3763e8ed59df.

15 Karabacak, Mert, and Konstantinos Margetis. 2023. "Embracing Large Language Models for Medical Applications: Opportunities and Challenges." Cureus. May 21, 2023. https://doi.org/10.7759/cureus.39305.

16 Bommasani, Rishi, Kevin Klyman, Daniel Zhang, and Percy Liang. 2023. "Stanford CRFM." Stanford University. June 15, 2023. https://crfm.stanford.edu/2023/06/15/eu-ai-act.html.

17 Bommasani, Rishi, Kevin Klyman, Daniel Zhang, and Percy Liang. 2023. "Stanford CRFM." Stanford University. June 15, 2023. https://crfm.stanford.edu/2023/06/15/eu-ai-act.html.

18 Bommasani, Rishi, Kevin Klyman, Daniel Zhang, and Percy Liang. 2023. "Stanford CRFM." Stanford University. June 15, 2023. https://crfm.stanford.edu/2023/06/15/eu-ai-act.html.

19 Gerrit De Vynck. 2023. "AI Learned from Their Work. Now They Want Compensation." *Washington Post*. July 16, 2023. https://www.washingtonpost.com/technology/2023/07/16/ai-programs-training-lawsuits-fair-use/.

20 Brittain, Blake. 2023. "US Judge Finds Flaws in Artists' Lawsuit against AI Companies." Reuters, July 19, 2023. https://www.reuters.com/legal/litigation/us-judge-finds-flaws-artists-lawsuit-against-ai-companies-2023-07-19/.

21 Knibbs, Kate. 2023. "The Battle over Books3 Could Change AI Forever." *Wired*. September 4, 2023. https://www.wired.com/story/battle-over-books3/.

22 Heath, Ryan. 2023. "AI Lawsuits Spread to Health." Axios. July 25, 2023. https://www.axios.com/2023/07/25/ai-lawsuits-health-cigna-algorithm-payment-denial.

23  Gates, Bill. 2023. "The Risks of AI Are Real but Manageable." GatesNotes: The Blog of Bill Gates. July 11, 2023. https://www.gatesnotes.com/The-risks-of-AI-are-real-but-manageable.

24 Sweenor, David. 2023. "GenAIOps: Evolving the

MLOps Framework." Medium. July 18, 2023. https://towardsdatascience.com/genaiops-evolving-the-mlops-framework-b0012f936379.

25  ai. 2023. "Power Requirements to Train Modern LLMs." nnlabs.org. March 5, 2023. https://www.nnlabs.org/power-requirements-of-large-language-models/.

26 C., David, and Paul J. 2023. "ChatGPT and Large Language Models: What's the Risk?" National Cyber Security Centre. March 14, 2023. https://www.ncsc.gov.uk/blog-post/chatgpt-and-large-language-models-whats-the-risk.

27 Bohannon, Molly. 2023. "Lawyer Used ChatGPT In Court—And Cited Fake Cases: A Judge Is Considering Sanctions." *Forbes*. June 8, 2023. https://www.forbes.com/sites/mollybohannon/2023/06/08/lawyer-used-chatgpt-in-court-and-cited-fake-cases-a-judge-is-considering-sanctions/?sh=47e03e697c7f.

28 "Moderation." OpenAI Platform. Accessed October 14, 2023. https://platform.openai.com/docs/guides/moderation/overview.

29 "Guardrail Metrics - Galileo." 2023. Rungalileo.io. 2023. https://docs.rungalileo.io/galileo/how-to-and-faq/ml-research-algorithms/guardrail-metrics.

30 Zou, Andy, Zifan Wang, J. Zico Kolter, and Matt Fredrikson. 2023. "Universal and Transferable Adversarial Attacks on Aligned Language Models." arXiv:2307.15043. July 27, 2023. https://doi.org/10.48550/arXiv.2307.15043.

31 Kahn, Jeremy. 2023. "Researchers Find a Way to Easily Bypass Guardrails on OpenAI's ChatGPT and All Other A.I. Chatbots." Yahoo Finance. July 28, 2023. https://finance.yahoo.com/news/researchers-way-easily-bypass-guardrails-183009628.html.

32 "Pricing." OpenAI. Accessed October 14, 2023. https://openai.com/pricing.